GULAM
DASTGEER

ईश्वर सहि

Made with ♥ on the Notion Press Platform
www.notionpress.com

*I am dedicating this book to the hard work of my younger brother Er.
Hardeep Singh by which he got success in his life.*

Contents

Foreword

Regardless of anything else, the fundamentals of social morality demand that each generation keep in mind all those people—both men and women—who, during their lives, contributed to the diversity of human society, heritage, polity, and overall nobility of ideas, making succeeding generations better than the previous ones. In this sense, politicians, scholars, and wise people all need our concern.

Ishwar Singh have more than ten years of experience in writing story books, sakhis of devotional saints and in research activities. He is a tremendous writer. He is doing excellent job by writing about Gulam Dastgeer. He had shown very keen interest in the field of cultural issues.

He is also a very excellent teacher and also having deep knowledge about the social science issues. I have always seen him working very hard for his various books. He just want to express about the Indian culture to our new generations in a simple and brief manner. I wish him all the very best for his new book.

Birinder Pal Kaur

Preface

This book describes the life of a man whose name is Gulam Dastgeer. How he spent his life in the harsh circumstances and his friends achieved success. What happened with that man in his school life? What was that wrong decision?

Acknowledgements

Writing a book is harder than I thought and more rewarding than I could have ever imagined. None of this would have been possible without my best friend, my teacher, my best motivator, my beloved mother Amarjit Kaur. She was the first who inspired me for my goals and taught me various subjects and created my interest specially in Social Sciences. She stood by me during every struggle and all my successes. Whatever I had achieved in my life it is due to my mother.

CHAPTER ONE

Gulam Dastgeer

Gulam Dastgeer excelled in school and was a high achiever. Due to his academic expertise in the subjects, he was also very well known among the teachers. He consistently achieved scores of over 90% in every subject. Ravi was one of Gulam Dastgeer's closest friends.

In the class, Ravi was a bright student as well. Gulam Dastgeer consistently placed first and Ravi came in second in school exams. Ravi, however, doesn't care about how he did on the school exams. He was pleased with his friend's success. They were both taking classes at the convent school. Gulam Dastgeer was awarded a scholarship by the school administration because of his outstanding academic performance.

Ravi and Gulam Dastgeer frequently attended school together. They were also neighbours. Their homes were located a vast distance from the school. But they never walked up to ask to ride the school bus. They both cherished going to school on foot. From his home, Ravi had no financial problems. His father was a successful businessman who owned several plots in the city's main market. The mother of Ravi was a private school teacher.

Gulam Dastgeer, on the other hand, came from a very underprivileged family. His father was a cobbler who operated a temporary shop on public property close to the city's bus terminal. Temporary implies that the shop was illegally occupying government property and that government officials could vandalise it at any time. Gulam Dastgeer's mother passed away when he was only two years old.

Because Ravi was aware of Gulam Dastgeer's family circumstances, he himself never rode the school bus to school. He accompanied Gulam Dastgeer as he travelled from his home to the school. Ravi used to always be there for Gulam Dastgeer when he appeared depressed because of his family's circumstances. Ravi occasionally bought books for Gulam Dastgeer and did his best to assist him.

One day Ravi made the sudden decision to leave school. Actually, Ravi's father made him to leave the school right away. Because of business losses, Ravi informed his best friend that his father was unwilling to remain in this city. His dad has made the decision to relocate to a big city. Gulam Dastgeer was astounded by the father of Ravi's rash choice. Gulam Dastgeer was feeling depressed at the time and kept quiet before breaking down in tears. Also sobbing in front of Gulam Dastgeer was Ravi. They were both very close friends who respected each other's emotions.

Ravi relocated to Surat in Gujarat with his family. One of Gujarat's largest cities, Surat is also crucial from a trade perspective. In order to establish a textile factory, Ravi's father invested the remaining funds along with him because he was interested in the textile industry. Because there was such a high demand for cotton textiles at the time on the global market, Ravi's father chose to do this. But a calculation went wrong.

The entire company was wiped out as a consequence of the world economic crisis. For the family of Ravi, these were extremely difficult years. Ravi enrolled in a nearby government school. He keeps going to the government school to study. Government schools in those days weren't in very good condition. Teachers frequently arrived to school late and left early. The majority of the time, principals of government schools are on leave. The same thing was going on at Ravi's school as well.

Ravi was extremely dissatisfied with the government school system, but he is currently without a backup plan. He was well aware of the dilemma facing his family. His mother was unemployed, and his father was struggling to grow his business. Ravi made the decision to tackle the challenges of government school. Although Ravi's first few days of school were challenging, he eventually adapted to the new environment.

With the classroom practice, Ravi demonstrated his abilities in front of his teachers. In all of the school's tests and exams, he consistently received high marks. Ravi was successful in projecting a positive image of a good student to his teachers. Maths captured Ravi's attention in a big way. He developed the ability to quickly and accurately answer every mathematical question. He had exceptional mathematical ability.

In those times, not all areas of the nation had access to electricity. The same issue of a lack of electricity existed in the neighbourhood where Ravi was renting a home to live with his family. Ravi used to study at night by the light of the Diwa (a handmade torch run on kerosene oil). The precise estimation of time during the night study presented another challenge. Back then, wall clocks and wrist watches were not prevalent. Ravi therefore planned his study according to the nearby factory's siren sound. After every two hours, the factory's siren blew. Whenever that siren rang, Ravi would come to know that now two hours have passed while studying. Ravi sometimes slept after two sirens and sometimes after three sirens.

Ravi advances his studies by putting in a lot of effort day and night. Ravi used to enter the competition first and always finished first whenever there was one at the school. Similar to this, Ravi received excellent grades in every class he did take. On the other hand, his father's company also began to prosper.

After successfully completing his 12th grade exams at the same public school, Ravi receives scholarship to pursue his graduate studies abroad. Since Ravi had a strong interest in mathematics from the start, he considered concentrating on it for the rest of his education. And he actually did that.

Now, a lot of time had passed. Additionally, Ravi had finished his courses. After finishing his studies abroad, Ravi is hired as an assistant professor at a top class university at Surat. After being offered the position of assistant professor, Ravi is overjoyed and immediately begins teaching young children. In the university, Ravi demonstrates his mettle as well as distinguishes himself from the other professors and students.

Ravi's parents are delighted to see how their son is progressing and hope to soon find a respectable woman to marry. In the morning, Ravi would work at the university, and in the evening, he would assist his father with his calculations. This is how a lot of time passed. Due to his talent, Ravi was also promoted within the university. He was appointed department chairman of mathematics.

One day, a quirk of timing forced Ravi to travel to the same city as his childhood friend in order to attend a seminar. who had the name Gulam Dastgeer. Ravi was equally eager to return to the same city and look for his friend.

When Ravi boards the train to travel to that city, he speculates along the way that Gulam Dastgeer must also be an adult and employed in a reputable position. Ravi was troubled by the possibility that the Gulam Dastgeer may not have left his house and gone somewhere else. The Gulam Dastgeer will have to return without seeing him if this occurs. Ravi became engrossed in his childhood memories while riding the train. He was thinking back to their earlier times playing and attending school together with the Gulam Dastgeer.

The train arrives in the same city the following day. Ravi notices that a lot has changed in this town as well when the train passes through. The city has grown significantly. The train arrives at the station shortly after, and Ravi begins getting ready to leave.

Finding a rickshaw so that he can get to the hotel is the first thing Ravi does after leaving the station. From a distance, Ravi makes a call to a rickshaw puller. The rickshaw puller soon appears in front of Ravi. The wind begins to blow on Ravi's face as soon as he sees the rickshaw puller's face. For a while, Ravi is completely speechless because the man pulling the rickshaw is the Gulam Dastgeer.

Ravi thinks to himself for a few moments that maybe no one helped the prince after I left this city. And perhaps the school has stopped his scholarship and he could not study further, due to which Gulam Dastgeer has come to the point of driving a rickshaw today.

Meanwhile, Gulam Dastgeer also recognizes Ravi but starts stealing eyes from Ravi. Ravi starts a conversation with Raj Kumar and asks him that you were very smart in studies, so why did you get down to driving a rickshaw?

Gulam Dastgeer does not respond to Ravi's words. Ravi then again asks Gulam Dastgeer whether the school had stopped your scholarship. Even if the scholarship had been stopped, why would you have not taken admission in a government school? The Gulam Dastgeer doesn't say anything again.

Then Ravi tells about himself, see, after studying in a government school, today I am working as the chairman of the mathematics department in the university. But why are you driving a rickshaw? When Ravi asks repeatedly, the Gulam Dastgeer starts crying bitterly.

Then Gulam Dastgeer tells Ravi that today I am in this condition because of some mistakes of my own. Otherwise I would have become a big man like you today. Ravi asks Raj Kumar that what mistake did you make that today you have to drive a rickshaw. Then Gulam Dastgeer tells Ravi that when we studied together in school, you were the only one from our class to participate in every competition. Because your way of speaking was very good and whenever you used to go on the stage and speak, you used to keep your words with great confidence.

But one day after you left, the teacher came to me and told me that now Ravi is not in the class, so you will have to participate in the coming function in place of Ravi. You have to address people on stage just like Ravi. Hearing this, the ground slipped from under my feet and I was very nervous because I had never spoken on stage before. The teacher wrote down my name and I started feeling very scared. I didn't go to school the day the function was supposed to happen and I was so scared that I couldn't muster up the courage to go to school after the function. It was my fear because of which I could not progress in life. The poverty in which I was born, I am still living in the same poverty.

Ravi feels very sorry after hearing these words of Gulam Dastgeer that I wish I could have been with him and could have made him understand that victory is not achieved by leaving the field. To win, one has to jump into the fray and then fight.

This story is based on a true incident which was narrated to me by my teacher. Today I have presented this story in front of you in the form of this small book. So that small children can realize the value of education in life. And never let your self-confidence weaken. If the self-confidence weakens, then do tell about it to your teachers and parents. Make sure to make any one teacher your mentor in life so that he can correct your thinking power from time to time.